SCIENTIFIC AMERICAN EDUCATIONAL PUBLISHING

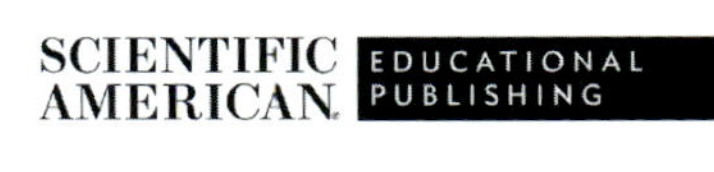

EARTH SCIENCE

10 FUN EARTH SCIENCE EXPERIMENTS

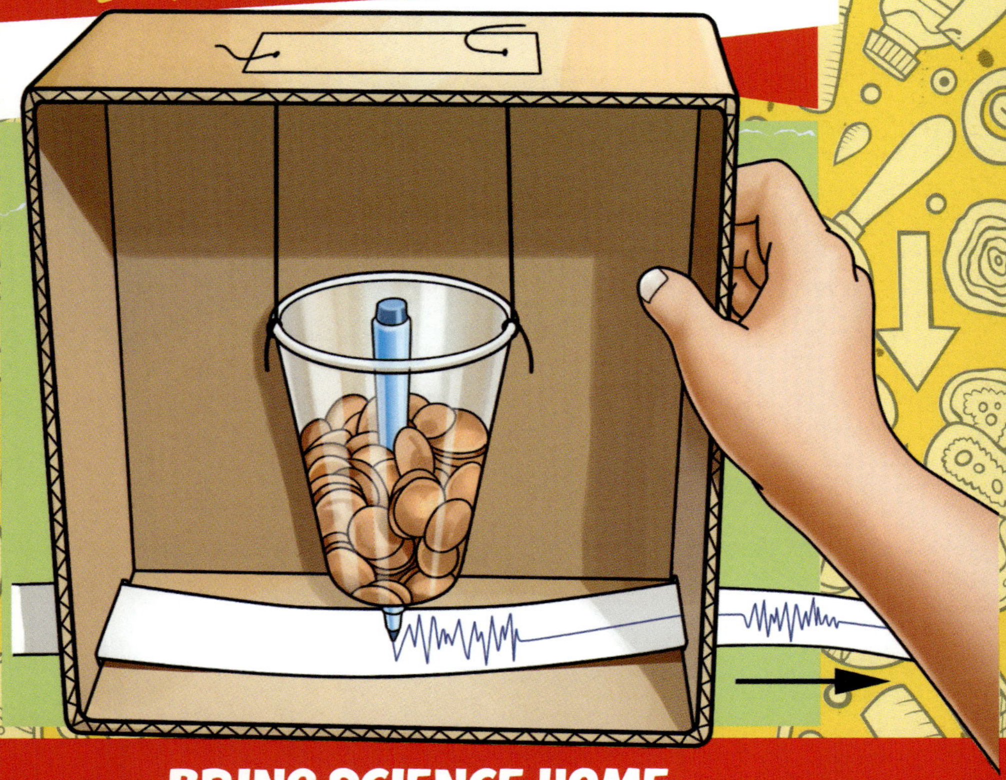

BRING SCIENCE HOME

Published in 2023 by The Rosen Publishing Group, Inc.
2544 Clinton St, Buffalo, NY 14224

First Edition

Editor: Kristen Nelson
Designer: Rachel Rising

Activity on page 5 by Science Buddies/Sabine De Brabandere (October 10, 2019); p. 11 by Science Buddies/ Ben Finio (August 22, 2019); p. 17 Science Buddies/Sabine De Brabandere (August 8, 2019); p. 23 by Science Buddies/Svenja Lohner (July 25, 2019); p. 29 by Science Buddies/Ben Finio (April 20, 2017); p. 35 by Science Buddies (April 30, 2015); p. 43 by Science Buddies (March 5, 2015); p. 49 by Exploratorium (January 15, 2015); p. 53 by Science Buddies (June 21, 2012); p. 57 by Science Buddies (March 1, 2012).

Photo Credits: pp. 4, 5, 11, 17, 23, 29, 35, 43, 49, 53, 57 Anna Frajtova/Shutterstock.com; pp. 9, 14, 17, 20, 26, 27, 32, 33, 40, 46, 47, 49, 51, 52, 56, 57, 59, 60 cve iv/Shutterstock.com.

All illustrations by Continuum Content Solutions

Cataloging-in-Publication Data
Names: Scientific American, inc.
Title: Earth science / edited by the Editors of Scientific American.
Description: Buffalo, New York : Scientific American Educational Publishing, 2023. | Series: Bring science home | Includes glossary and index.
Identifiers: ISBN 9781684169726 (pbk.) | ISBN 9781684169733 (library bound) | ISBN 9781684169740 (ebook)
Subjects: LCSH: Earth sciences--Experiments--Juvenile literature. | Science projects--Juvenile literature.
Classification: LCC QE29.E378 2023 | DDC 550.78--dc23

Manufactured in the United States of America

Some of the images in this book illustrate individuals who are models. The depictions do not imply actual situations or events.

CPSIA Compliance Information: Batch #SACS23. For further information contact Rosen Publishing at 1-800-237-9932.

CONTENTS

Introduction 4

Sweet Earthquake Structure Shake 5

Shaky Science: Build a Seismograph 11

Weathering Rocks ⚛ 17

Make Water Disappear—with the Wet-Sand Effect 23

Earthquake Rollers 29

Cartography: Flattening Earth 35

Soil Science: How Moist Is That Mud? 43

Salt Sculpture Stalactites ⚛ 49

Shoreline Science: Exploring the Erosive Energy of Waves 53

Rock Solid? How Particles Affect Porosity ⚛ 57

The Scientific Method 61

Glossary 62

Additional Resources 63

Index 64

⚛ THESE ACTIVITIES INCLUDE SCIENCE FAIR PROJECT IDEAS.

INTRODUCTION

Earth science includes the study of soil, weather, the environment, and how living things interact with Earth. Using materials you can often find around your home and garden, you will investigate erosion, earthquakes, mapmaking, and the effect of pressure on wet sand in the following experiments—and so much more! Get ready; get set; experiment!

Projects marked with ⚛ include a section called Science Fair Project ideas. These ideas can help you develop your own original science fair project. Science fair judges tend to reward creative thought and imagination, and it helps if you are really interested in your project. You will also need to follow the scientific method. See page 61 for more information about that.

Sweet Earthquake Structure Shake

THE GROUND IS SOLID—UNTIL IT'S NOT! LEARN ABOUT WHAT CAN HAPPEN DURING AN EARTHQUAKE BY BUILDING A SWEET AND STICKY STRUCTURE AND GIVING IT A SHAKE.

Have you ever thought about what type of ground buildings are constructed on? Rock, gravel, sand, soil, and many others—there are lots of different types of "ground." This issue becomes especially important in areas that are likely to get earthquakes. In this activity, you will build a sweet building on a homemade shake table and find out how an earthquake impacts buildings constructed on sand. How will your structure perform in a model earthquake?

PROJECT TIME

45-60 minutes

KEY CONCEPTS

Physics
Geology
Earthquakes
Engineering
Materials

BACKGROUND

Earth's outer layer is like a puzzle made up of huge pieces of land. These pieces are called the tectonic plates, and they slide around slowly on the surface of the globe; they push against and slide alongside one another. Sometimes this friction generates sudden movements, which can trigger earthquakes. Earthquakes release a lot of energy, which is radiated out in the form of waves called seismic waves. One type of wave pushes and pulls the material it moves through, and people feel it as a back-and-forth or side-to-side motion. This type of wave is called the primary or P-wave. A P-wave can move through solid and liquid material.

The type of ground you stand on as seismic waves pass by also affects what you feel. Soft soils such as sand tend to amplify the shaking, compared with hard soils such as bedrock. In addition to being soft, sand can also undergo a "liquefaction process" during an earthquake. This means the sand can change from behaving like a solid to behaving like a thick liquid, which further amplifies shaking.

In this activity, you will construct a building and place it on material that mimics sand. You will test it on a homemade shake table that generates movement resembling the pushing and pulling of a P-wave. How well will your building withstand the quake?

MATERIALS

- Butcher paper or newspaper
- Wax paper
- Damp cloth
- Starburst candy or sugar cubes (40 or more)
- No-stir peanut butter or a substitute, such as soy butter or sunflower seed butter
- Spoon or butter knife
- Cornstarch
- Water
- Measuring cup
- Shallow box
- Marbles or any small balls identical in size (1 to 2 dozen)
- Shallow tray that is a few inches smaller than your shallow box. (Aluminum cake trays work well.)
- Fork
- Yellow food coloring (optional)
- Play-Doh (optional)
- Grape-Nuts cereal (optional)
- Additional trays (optional)

PREPARATION

- Protect your work area with butcher paper or newspaper. This will speed up cleanup time. Have a wet cloth ready to wipe off your hands when they get too sticky.
- Place a square of wax paper at least 5 inches by 5 inches (12.7 cm by 12.7 cm) in front of you.
- Unwrap the Starburst candies, and open the peanut butter jar. The candies will be the bricks of your structure; the peanut butter will serve as the mortar that keeps the bricks together.
- Scoop up a little peanut butter with a spoon, a butter knife, or a finger. Apply it to the side of a candy and stick another candy against it. Repeat this process to build a building. You can build any structure you like, but it needs to fit well inside your tray.
- Cut the wax paper so there is about 1 to 2 inches (2.5 to 5 cm) of paper left on each side of the building. Set the building aside on the wax paper until you are ready to test it.
- To prepare the mixture that will mimic the reaction of sand during an earthquake, scoop 3 cups of cornstarch into the shallow tray, and add 1 1/2 cups (355 ml) of water. Add a few drops of yellow food coloring if available. Use a fork or your hands to mix it well. Getting the right consistency of the cornstarch mixture is important. It should be firm enough to support your test building—but still liquid enough that it slowly oozes down your fork or fingers when you scoop it up. Add more cornstarch if it is too liquid, or add more water if it is too firm. Set aside.
- To assemble your shake table, place the shallow box in front of you. Put the marbles into the box, and set the tray with the cornstarch mixture so that it is resting on top of the marbles. When you shake the box, the tray should sway back and forth or side to side as it rolls over the marbles.

PROCEDURE

- Practice shaking your shake table. Shake it quickly, but gently enough and with the right-sized motions so that the tray does not hit the sides of the box.
- Use the wax paper to carefully place your building on top of the cornstarch mixture. Look closely. Your building should sit on the cornstarch with only the wax paper in between, but it should not sink in. It is fine if your building makes a print in the mixture—similar to a footprint in wet sand. If it slowly sinks all the way down, however, your mixture is too wet. Remove your building on the wax paper, mix in more cornstarch, and try again.
- *What do you think will happen to your structure when you shake the box quickly?*
- Shake the box fast enough so the tray with the cornstarch mixture sways back and forth but does not hit the side of the box. As you shake the box, count to 20 before you take a break to observe. *Has the building changed in any way? Can you see signs of cracks? Did the building sink deeper into the mixture?*
- *What do you think will happen if you shake with more force—or for a longer time?*
- Try it out! Gradually increase the force with which you shake the box, making sure not to let the tray hit the side of the box. Look at the cornstarch mixture while you shake. *Can you see it moving almost like a very thick liquid?*
- Assess the damage. *Is your structure still standing? Did the building or the debris sink deep into the mixture, or is it standing or laying on top of it? Why would this happen?*
- Push a finger into the mixture. *Does the mixture feel firm?*

- Keep pushing while you shake the box vigorously with your other hand. *Does your finger sink in the mixture? Does it feel like being in a very thick liquid? Why would that be?*

EXTRA

Use different materials to mimic different soil types, and use your shake table to see which soil types hold up a building best. Play-Doh can model bedrock, Grape-Nuts cereal can reproduce gravel, and a mixture of two to three parts of Grape-Nuts cereal with one part of water works well to mimic loose soil. Repeat the procedure with each of these soil types. Test identical buildings, and keep the strength and duration of your shaking consistent. *Would some soils make the shaking generated by a P-wave more intense than others?*

Test different designs of structures. Keep the strength and duration of your shaking the same, and do not change the soil type, but try an alternative building design. *Would a tall building be more vulnerable? Would it be better to have a large surface area, or would smaller buildings withstand the shaking generated by a P-wave better?*

OBSERVATIONS AND RESULTS

Did the cornstarch mixture become a thick liquid after being vigorously shaken?

The cornstarch mixture acts like a solid when it is left alone, but it behaves more like a thick liquid when vigorously shaken. You could see and feel that it was like a solid at first, as it could hold the building, and you could feel the mixture resist your finger when you pushed on it. Shaking changed that. The building or its debris probably sank into the mixture while you shook the box—just like it would sink in thick mud. You could likely also feel the mixture giving way for your finger when you shook the box while pushing on the mixture—just like it would in a thick liquid.

Sand acts in a similar way. At rest, it behaves like a solid, but when shaken forcefully, it acts more like a thick liquid. Scientists call this the liquefaction process, and earthquakes are known to set this process in action.

The shake table in this activity recreates the side-to-side or back-and-forth movement created by a P-wave during an earthquake. However, a real seismic wave generates more powerful movement. You didn't use real sand for this activity because you are trying to model the process by which sand changes from acting like a solid to acting like a liquid when it is shaken in an earthquake. With your hand-powered shake table, you cannot shake sand fast enough to achieve liquefaction, so you used a cornstarch mixture instead.

If you tested other "ground" materials (such as Grape-Nuts or Play-Doh), you might have seen different results after shaking. Based on what you tested, what type of ground would you build a structure on in an earthquake-prone area? In most areas where earthquakes are common, engineers use many other strategies to help buildings withstand shaking.

CLEANUP

Throw away your cornstarch-and-water mixture with the trash. Do not pour it down the drain, as it will clog the pipes. Put away other materials used in the experiment.

Shaky Science
Build a Seismograph

LEARN HOW TO MEASURE MOVEMENT WITH SOME SIMPLE PHYSICS BY BUILDING YOUR VERY OWN SEISMOGRAPH—AND SHAKE IT UP!

Scientists study earthquakes so we can understand and predict them better. In this activity, you will learn about one of the tools scientists use to measure the strength of an earthquake—and build your own machine using simple materials.

PROJECT TIME

30-45 minutes

KEY CONCEPTS

Physics
Engineering
Earthquakes
Measurement

BACKGROUND

Earthquakes happen all the time, but most of them are so small that we can't feel them, and they don't cause any damage. Large earthquakes, however, can be catastrophic—causing significant damage to property and loss of life. An earthquake's strength is measured on what is called the Richter scale. The Richter scale goes from 1 to 10. Each increase of 1 on the Richter scale means the earthquake is actually 10 times more powerful (for example a 2.0 earthquake is 10 times stronger than a 1.0 earthquake—not twice as strong). As of 2022, the strongest earthquake ever recorded measured 9.5 on the Richter scale.

Scientists use a machine called a seismograph to measure the motion of the ground during an earthquake. Seismographs are very sensitive and can detect earthquakes that occur very far away (along with other things that make the ground shake, such as volcanic eruptions or large explosions) that might be too faint for humans to feel. Seismographs are made by hanging a heavy weight from a rigid frame connected to the ground. When the ground moves during an earthquake, the frame moves back and forth along with the ground. The heavy weight, however, is not connected directly to the ground, and it wants to stay in place. The result is that the weight holds still, while the frame moves back and forth around it. By placing a pen on the weight and paper on the frame, scientists can see the relative motion of the weight and frame through the markings, which create a seismogram. The seismogram can be analyzed later to find out when an earthquake happened and how strong it was. Modern seismographs record this motion as an electrical signal, but in this activity, you will build your own old-fashioned seismograph that uses a marker to record an "earthquake" on a paper strip.

MATERIALS

- Medium-sized cardboard box
- Paper or plastic disposable cup
- String
- Marker
- Scissors (have an adult help cut the cardboard and cup if needed)
- Paper or a very long printed receipt from a store
- Tape
- Coins, marbles, small rocks, or other small, heavy objects to use as weights
- Another person to help
- Graphing paper (optional)

PREPARATION

- Carefully cut the lid or flaps off the cardboard box. Stand the box up on one of the smaller sides.
- Carefully poke two holes opposite from each other near the rim of the cup.
- Tie a piece of string (slightly longer than the length of the box) to each hole.
- Carefully poke two holes in the top of the box (make them the same distance apart as the holes in the cup).
- Push the two pieces of string through the box holes, and tie them together above the top of the box so the cup hangs down inside the box. The bottom of the cup should be about 1 inch (2.5 cm) above the bottom of the box.
- Carefully poke a hole in the center of the bottom of the cup. Remove the cap from the marker, and push the marker through the hole so its tip just barely touches the bottom of the box.
- Fill the cup with coins or other small weights. *Why do you think the weights are important?*
- Fold a piece of paper in half lengthwise, then fold it in half again. Unfold the paper, and cut along the folds to form four equal-size strips. Tape the strips of paper together end to end to form one long strip. (If you have a long, printed receipt, you can skip this step.)
- Carefully cut two slits on opposite sides of the cardboard box—as close as possible to the bottom edge. The slits should be wide enough to pass the paper strip through one side, across the middle of the box, and out the other side.
- Make sure the marker is centered on the paper strip. You might need to poke different holes in the top of the box and re-hang the cup if necessary.

PROCEDURE

- Now you are finally ready to use your seismograph! Stabilize the box with your hands as your helper slowly starts to slowly pull the paper strip through the box from side to side. *What does the marker draw on the paper strip?*
- Now, shake the box back and forth as your helper continues to pull the paper strip through, doing their best to pull at a constant speed. *How does the line on the paper strip change?*
- Pause your shaking for a few seconds, then try shaking the box harder.
- Pause for a few more seconds, then shake the box very gently.
- Pull the paper strip all the way out of the box, and look at the line. *Can you tell how hard the box was shaking based on the line? Can you tell when the box was not shaking at all?*
- Repeat with additional strips of paper as you test out different shaking amounts.

EXTRA

Does your seismograph work if you shake the box side-to-side or up and down? Can you design a seismograph that can record motion in multiple directions?

EXTRA

Can you design your own scale for measuring the strength of your "earthquakes"? Try using graph paper, and see how different amounts of shaking measure up on your scale.

OBSERVATIONS AND RESULTS

When your helper pulls the paper through the box with no shaking, the marker should just draw a straight line on the paper. When you shake the box, it moves back and forth, and the paper moves along with it. Because of the heavy mass of the cup and the way it is suspended by strings, the cup does not move as much. This means that the paper moves back and forth under the (mostly) stationary marker, resulting in a squiggly line. The size of these squiggles (called their amplitude) corresponds to how hard you shook the box—just like how the line drawn by a real seismograph corresponds to the strength of the earthquake.

CLEANUP

Recycle the paper and box you used.
Put away all other materials used.

Weathering Rocks

HOW DOES ROCK WEATHER THE AGES? LEARN ABOUT THESE PHYSICAL AND CHEMICAL PROCESSES WITH A LITTLE SWEET SCIENCE!

Have you ever visited a canyon or cave and wondered how those formations came to be? Or observed smooth stones by a river or beach? These results are due to a process called weathering. Weathering, or the wearing-away of rock by exposure to the elements, not only creates smooth rocks as well as caves and canyons, but it also slowly eats away at other hard objects, including some statues and buildings. Try this process out on a sugar cube and feel how powerful weathering can be.

PROJECT TIME

20-30 minutes

KEY CONCEPTS

Geology
Weathering
Physics
Chemistry

BACKGROUND

Rock might seem permanent, but it is actually constantly being broken down. We often do not notice this process because it happens so slowly. As soon as rock is exposed to the elements, it can start being broken down through the process of weathering. Scientists categorize this process into two groups: physical weathering and chemical weathering.

Physical weathering (also called mechanical weathering) happens when physical forces repeatedly act on the rock. One example is rocks tumbling over one another, knocking off pieces from one another. This often happens in a river or desert, or on a hillside.

In chemical weathering, the rock disintegrates or even dissolves because a chemical reaction changes the composition of the rock. When certain types of rock come into contact with rainwater (which is often slightly acidic, especially when there is pollution present), a chemical reaction occurs, slowly transforming the rock into substances that dissolve in water. As these substances dissolve, they get washed away. It is almost as if the rock has vanished!

In this activity, you will model physical and chemical weathering with sugar cubes—so you can see it happen before your eyes.

MATERIALS

- At least four sugar cubes
- Water
- Dark colored paper or countertop
- Glass
- Dropper
- Work area that can get wet
- Towel for cleaning up (optional)
- Clay (optional)
- Spray bottle (optional)
- Frosting (optional)
- Nail file (optional)
- Tray or large dish with sides (optional)

PREPARATION

- Gather your materials in a location that can get wet.

PROCEDURE

- Think of a few ways you can break or pulverize your rock (sugar cube) with mechanical weathering.
- Try it out with one of your sugar cubes!
- *Did you crush it, smash it, or apply another force on it? Can you list examples of how rocks get smashed or crushed in nature?*
- Now take two new sugar cubes, and grind one against the other over a dark colored piece of paper or countertop. *What happens? Do you see sugar dust on the paper or countertop? What is happening to your rock (sugar cube)?*
- Try rounding the edges of your sugar cube this way. *Does it work?*
- Look back at what is left of your sugar cube. *What does it look like? Is it still sugar?*
- Now take a new sugar cube. *What are some ways you could break down your rock (sugar cube) with chemical weathering?*
- In this activity, we'll use water drops to simulate rain. Place the sugar cube in a glass.
- Fill your dropper with water, and squeeze a few drops on the sugar cube. Look and feel to observe what happens.

- *What do you think will happen if you drop more water on the sugar cube? What do you think would happen if you drop 10 or 100 (or more) drops on the sugar cube? Will it still be a sugar cube? Will it still be sugar?*
- Drop more water on your sugar cube. *Where does the sugar go? Can you make the cube disappear completely?*

SCIENCE FAIR IDEA

Place a few sugar cubes in a glass. Cover them with clay. The sugar cubes represent a layer of rock, and the clay represents topsoil. Make a few holes or a crack in the clay so rainwater can seep into the ground and reach the layer of rock. Spray water over your glass, representing rain coming down over your piece of land. *What do you think will happen to your layer of rock? Might caves form? How does this process depend on having different types of materials in the ground?*

SCIENCE FAIR IDEA

Make a sugar-cube sculpture or structure. To glue cubes together, wet one side of the cube and press it against another cube. If you need stronger glue, frosting can do the trick. Make sure your sculpture has some details and sharp edges. A nail file can help you sculpt the cubes. *What do you think will happen to your sculpture when it is exposed to rain?* Place your sculpture on a tray or dish with sides, and use a spray bottle to let it rain over your sculpture. First a little—then more. *What happens?* Look carefully at the details and edges: *Do they change? What will happen eventually after a lot of rain?* This is exactly what acidic rain can do to some statues and buildings over time.

OBSERVATIONS AND RESULTS

Was breaking a sugar cube by smashing, crushing, or grinding it easy? Rock breaks down in a similar way—but a lot more slowly—in nature in this process of physical or mechanical weathering. Forces in nature, such as gravity, wind, and even the push of freezing water or plant roots, impact rocks. These forces eventually wear the rock down. The result is smaller pieces of rock—just like you were left with smaller pieces of sugar.

What about your chemical weathering test? Did the sugar cube become weak and eventually dissolve in the drops of water? That happens to some types of rock, too. Some minerals in rock react with liquids or gases, creating new substances, which are often weaker—and sometimes even dissolve in water. After you applied enough water, you probably did not have any sugar cube left as it was carried away with the water. In a similar way, rocks can dissolve and be washed away, forming caves.

If you tried to build a sugar statue and exposed it to water, you probably saw it slowly disappear. This happens to some statues and buildings—and at a faster rate when more pollution makes the rain more acidic.

CLEANUP

Throw away any leftover used sugar. Pour out water used. Put away all other materials used.

Make Water Disappear with the Wet-Sand Effect

CAN YOU SQUEEZE MORE WATER INTO WET SAND? LEARN ABOUT A PARTICULARITY OF PARTICLES WITH THIS GRANULAR PHYSICS ACTIVITY!

Summer is a nice time to take a stroll at the beach and walk barefoot along the shoreline. While doing that, have you ever looked at your footprints in the wet sand? If so, you might have noticed that with every step it looks like the sand around your feet dries out. Why is that? These dry footprints are caused by the pressure of your feet. You will find out exactly how this happens by trying this beachy activity!

PROJECT TIME

30-45 minutes

KEY CONCEPTS

Physics
Materials
Compression
Geology

BACKGROUND

Many beaches are made of sand, which comes from rocks that have been ground into tiny particles by water and wind. Materials such as sand that are made of many separate tiny particles are called granular materials. Even when sand particles appear to be directly touching each other, because they are irregularly shaped, there are tiny spaces in between them. (Think about how a pile of larger rocks has similar spaces between them.) These spaces are called pores. There are many pores between all the sand particles at the beach.

If you pour water on the sand, the water seems to disappear into the sand. It doesn't actually disappear—it drains into the tiny pores between the grains. Once all these pores are filled with water, the sand is saturated, which means that the sand cannot take up any more water. When you squeeze this saturated sand, you would probably expect the water in the sand to come out of the pores again, similar to what happens when you squeeze a wet sponge. However, this is not what happens. The exact opposite is the case. More water seems to disappear into the sand! The reason for this is something called dilatancy of granular materials.

Dilatancy means that a material expands when you squeeze it (put it under pressure) instead of contracting. This happens because under pressure, the sand grains actually push each other slightly farther apart, which makes more space between them. This means there is more space for water to flow into, resulting in a dry footprint on the beach. Once the pressure is released, the sand grains settle closer together again, leaving less room for water. In this activity, you will demonstrate this wet-sand effect—and you don't even have to be at the beach!

MATERIALS

- Bowl
- Sand
- Water bottle (narrow mouth)
- Two large balloons (ideally they will be transparent)
- Two transparent straws
- Two rubber bands
- Paper
- Spoon
- Water
- Towel
- Workspace that can tolerate spills
- Wide-mouthed plastic water bottle (optional)
- Ruler (optional)
- Tape (optional)

- Permanent marker (optional)
- C-clamp (optional)
- Two pieces of scrap wood (optional)

PREPARATION

- Use the piece of paper to make a funnel, and place the funnel into the mouth of the narrow-mouth water bottle. Then spoon the sand into the paper funnel, filling the water bottle all the way up with dry sand.
- Inflate one of the balloons. Then stretch the balloon's neck over the mouth of the water bottle. Flip the bottle upside down, and pour the sand into the balloon.
- Once all the sand is in the balloon, remove the balloon from the bottle, and let the remaining air out. The balloon should now be filled with sand only.
- Add water to the sand inside the balloon until the sand is saturated and cannot absorb any more water. (You can use the same inverted bottle technique that you used for the sand.) The sand inside the balloon should look darker from all sides once it is saturated with water. *Where does the water go when you pour it on the sand?*
- When the sand is saturated, insert a straw far enough into the neck of the balloon so that the end of the straw is in the wet sand. Attach the straw tightly in place with a rubber band around the neck of the balloon.
- Fill the second balloon with water. Then insert the second straw into the neck of the balloon so that the end of the straw is in the water. Again, attach the straw tightly with a rubber band.

PROCEDURE

- Hold the balloon filled with water at its neck where it is connected to the straw. Hold it over the bowl in case it spills. Then add water to the straw until it is filled halfway. *What do you think will happen to the water in the straw when you squeeze the balloon?*
- Squeeze the balloon slightly with your hands. Observe the water inside the straw. *What happens to the water inside the straw? Did you expect this to happen?*
- Put the water-filled balloon aside and pick up the sand-filled balloon. Again, add water to the straw until it is filled up halfway. *What do you expect to happen this time when you squeeze the balloon?*
- Squeeze the balloon with both hands as much as you can. Observe what happens to the water inside the straw while you compress the saturated sand. *Does the water level in the straw rise, fall, or stay the same? Can you explain your observations?*
- Now release the pressure on the balloon and shake it slightly while observing the water level in the straw. *Does the water level change again? How?*

EXTRA

Try a simpler version of this activity. Add sand to a wide-mouthed plastic water bottle until it is three-quarters full. Add water until the sand is saturated and you have about 1/4 inch of water (0.6 cm) standing on top of the sand. Then squeeze the water bottle with your hands. *What do you notice?* While squeezing, turn the water bottle upside down over a bowl. *Do you see water dripping into the bowl when inverting the bottle?* Then stop squeezing the bottle and shake it slightly. *What happens?* Now turn the water bottle upside down without squeezing it. *Does water get into the bowl this time?*

What other granular materials can you use to demonstrate the wet sand effect? Try clay, glass stones, or "magic sand." *Do you get similar results?*

EXTRA

Try to quantify how much water disappears into the sand depending on the pressure you apply to the balloon. Hold a ruler next to the straw and make marks every 1/4 inch (0.6 cm) with a permanent marker. Then instead of using your hands to apply pressure to the balloon, use a C-clamp that you wrap around the middle of the balloon. To apply pressure to a larger area of the balloon, you can put a piece of scrap wood on each side of the balloon before you attach the C-clamp. Write down how much the water level changes with every turn of the C-clamp screw.

OBSERVATIONS AND RESULTS

When you squeezed the water-filled balloon, you probably saw water rise up the straw as you expected. When you squeezed the sand-filled balloon, however, the water level probably went down, which seems counterintuitive. This happens because under pressure the sand particles pushed each other farther apart, making the sand expand in volume. This creates more pore space between the sand particles, which the water inside the straw can drain into.

When you release the pressure on the sand and shake the balloon a little bit, the sand particles go back into their previous, denser arrangement. As a result, the water inside the straw starts to slowly rise again as the pore space between the sand particles decreases. This is exactly what happens when you make a dry footprint on wet sand. As your foot applies pressure to the saturated sand underneath, the grains of sand move, which creates more pore space for the water to disappear in. The sand around your foot appears dry. When you remove your foot—and the pressure on the sand—the water comes back out of the sand.

CLEANUP

Remove the water from the water-filled balloon and dispose of both balloons, including the straws, in your regular trash.

Earthquake Rollers

SHAKE IT UP! USE PHYSICS TO SEE HOW YOU CAN MINIMIZE MOVEMENT DURING A TABLETOP EARTHQUAKE.

Earthquakes can cause damage to buildings and be dangerous to people. However, some of the world's most populous cities are in earthquake-prone regions. How can engineers keep the millions of people in those cities safe? Find out how you can use science to save lives in this fun activity!

PROJECT TIME

30-45 minutes

KEY CONCEPTS

Physics
Engineering
Earthquakes

BACKGROUND

Earth's tectonic plates are continuously moving. Usually this movement is very slow—so slow that we can barely notice it. This slow movement may eventually cause cracks to form in buildings over time but will usually not cause sudden, unexpected damage. Sometimes, however, the plates get stuck for awhile and then rapidly become "unstuck"—kind of like when you try to open a stuck window when at first it doesn't move at all and then suddenly moves very fast. We call this sudden movement of the ground an earthquake. These events can cause buildings to wobble and even collapse, posing a serious danger to the people inside or near them.

Engineers have developed methods to make buildings more earthquake-resistant. For example, some buildings are slightly flexible so they can wobble back and forth a bit without breaking. Some very tall buildings have a heavy weight at the top called a tuned mass damper that helps cancel out the vibrations from a quake. Other buildings have isolation bearings, also referred to as a base isolation system. As the name implies, these bearings help isolate the base of a building from the ground, allowing it to move independently during an earthquake—that is, as the ground moves back and forth, the structure does not move with it. The concept is similar to shock absorbers on a car. When you ride over a big speed bump or pothole in the road, the shock absorbers help prevent the vibration from being transferred to the passengers in the car.

Engineers test their earthquake-resistant designs on model buildings using shake tables—special tables that shake back and forth to simulate an earthquake. In this project, you will use a simple hand-powered shake table to demonstrate how isolation bearings can help prevent a building from shaking back and forth with the ground during an earthquake

MATERIALS

- Small cardboard box
- Piece of corrugated cardboard, larger than the base of the box
- Scissors
- Tape
- Several round markers or crayons
- Pen or pencil
- Piece of paper
- Flat desk or table next to a wall
- Ruler

PREPARATION

- Carefully cut two or three small squares from the piece of cardboard, and tape them together.
- Tape the cardboard squares to the wall about 1 foot (30.5 cm) above your desk or table.
- Tape the top edge of the piece of paper to the cardboard squares so the paper hangs down with a gap between it and the wall. Allow the paper to hang freely—do not tape its other edges to the wall.
- Use the pen and ruler to make a bold mark in the middle of one lower edge of the cardboard box.
- Tape the pen to the top of the cardboard box, so its point hangs over the edge.

PROCEDURE

- Place the cardboard box in front of the piece of paper you attached to the wall, with the point of the pen lightly touching the paper.
- Tape the ruler to the table in front of the box.
- Practice shaking the box side to side a few times.
- The pen should press against the paper hard enough that it draws a horizontal line when you shake the box. If it does not draw a line, try adjusting the distance of the box from the wall or try a different writing instrument (such as a different pen, or a pencil or marker) to see if that works better.
- Using the ruler and the center mark you drew on the box, try to consistently shake the box back and forth the same distance (for example, by 1/2 inch [1.2 cm] in each direction). Keeping this distance and the speed at which you shake the box constant is important for your tests.

- Now, try placing the box on top of several round markers, on top of a piece of cardboard. The markers should be perpendicular to the wall.
- Shake the piece of cardboard back and forth, the same distance and speed you shook the box itself. *What do you notice about the box's movement? Does the mark the pen makes on the paper change?*

EXTRA

You just demonstrated a very simple base isolation system, but it has room for improvement. For example, you might notice it is hard to keep the box centered and it tends to drift to one side and fall off the markers. *Can you design a system to keep the box centered and make it return to its original location or prevent it from sliding off the edge of the cardboard?* For example, try using rubber bands attached to the cardboard base and sides of the building or build padded stoppers with cotton balls on the cardboard base.

The background section mentions some other ways to make a building earthquake-resistant. You can try building an earthquake-resistant tower. (For example, you can use building toys such as LEGO or K'Nex, or craft materials such as Popsicle sticks and glue or wooden skewers and Styrofoam balls.) *Can you make the tower flexible so it bends but does not break during a simulated earthquake? Can you add a tuned mass damper to your tower to decrease how much it vibrates?* (Search online for videos showing how tuned mass dampers work.)

Even with a ruler, consistently shaking your building by hand can be difficult. You can build a simple rubber band-powered shake table that allows you to do more controlled, repeatable shaking.

OBSERVATIONS AND RESULTS

You should notice the cardboard box does not move back and forth as much when you place it on the markers. This is because the round markers allow the box and the ground to slide back and forth with respect to each other. When you shake the cardboard, it moves back and forth under the box—but this motion is not completely transferred to the box. (Some motion is still transferred due to friction in the rollers.) This simulates a base isolation system that lets a building move side to side independently of the ground.

Real-life base isolation systems are more complicated than this. As mentioned in the "extra" step on page 32, you might have noticed that it was hard to get your building to return to exactly where it started. It might tend to drift off to one side and fall off the markers. Obviously that would not be acceptable with a real building—you need it to stay in the same place! Real base isolation systems contain springs, which generate a restoring force to pull the structure back toward the middle when it moves to either side. This introduces a new problem, however—springs oscillate (think of a Slinky bouncing back and forth after you pull on one end). So, base isolation systems also include dampers, or elements that use friction to diminish the oscillations. You might be able to build a better base isolation system using household materials. However, be careful—strong springs (such as tightly pulled rubber bands) with too little friction can actually make the oscillations worse!

CLEANUP

Recycle the box, cardboard, and paper used. Put away all other materials.

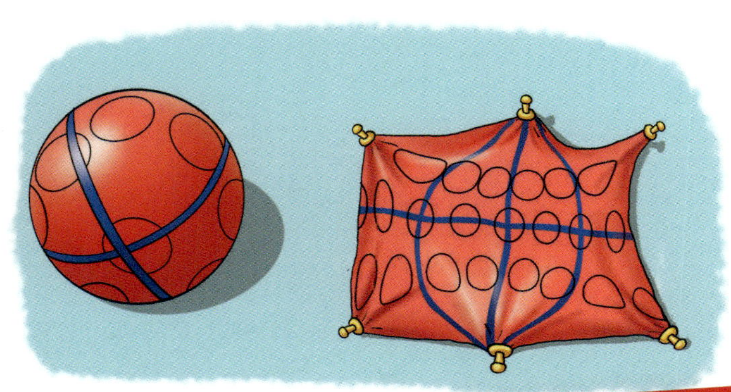

Cartography
Flattening Earth

SCIENTISTS KNOW THAT EARTH IS ROUND—AND MAKING FLAT MAPS OF IT IS A CHALLENGE! FIND OUT HOW IT CAN BE DONE IN THIS ACTIVITY.

Have you ever spent time looking at a world map and imagined traveling to distant locations? Maybe you see yourself drawing your own map of your new discoveries and your journeys along the way. However, Earth itself is round, so how do you create an accurate flat map? Throughout history, cartographers around the world have found different methods for creating flat maps of Earth. None can represent reality exactly, but each is useful for specific purposes. Try this activity and see how cartographers today could have helped explorers of the past!

PROJECT TIME

30-45 minutes

KEY CONCEPTS

Earth Science
Maps
Cartography

BACKGROUND

Creating a map of a small area might be relatively easy; making a flat map of the full Earth, however, is a completely different challenge. Cartographers (mapmakers) have found various ways to create flat maps of the world. These are called projections. How do they do it? There are several ways it can be done, but every type of projection distorts reality in some way. Scientists use a Tissot's indicatrix to quantify distortions that are introduced when creating a map. You will do something similar in this activity. You will draw identically sized circles all over your "Earth" (a balloon), create a projection similar to a type of projection called a Mercator projection, and study how the circles are distorted in area, shape, and distance on the flat map. You will be surprised how your circles look on your flat map!

MATERIALS

- Surface covered with butcher paper or other protective material
- Medium-size balloon (for example, a 12-inch [30.5 cm] balloon)
- Bottle cap (such as one from a plastic water bottle)
- Permanent marker (medium-thick works best)
- Scissors
- Six pushpins
- Cardboard piece, 8 by 10 inches (20 by 25 cm) or larger (It should be either thick cardboard or two layers of regular cardboard so the pushpins do not stick through.)
- Two assistants (The activity can be done alone but is easier with assistants.)

PREPARATION

- You will use a balloon to represent Earth in this activity. Blow up the balloon to about half full and tie it. The top of the balloon and the knot represent the North and South Poles, respectively.

- If you would like, use the permanent marker and label the top of the balloon with an "N" and the knot with an "S." This will remind you where each pole is located.
- Draw an equator on the balloon with permanent marker. Earth's equator is an imaginary line around its center, which is equidistant (the same distance) from the North Pole and the South Pole. (Note: Once your marker lines are drawn, always set the balloon on the butcher paper or on the cardboard to avoid getting dirty prints on your work surface.)
- Draw four equally spaced lines of longitude on the balloon with permanent marker. Lines of longitude are imaginary lines running over the globe, connecting the North Pole with the South Pole. They are perpendicular (at a right angle) to the equator.
- Look: *How is this balloon similar to a real globe? How is it different from a real globe?*

PROCEDURE

- Inspired by methods used by scientists (like Tissot's indicatrix method), you will draw same-size circles all over the globe (balloon), create a projection (flat map), and study its distortions.
- Start by drawing one circle centered on an intersection of the equator and a line of longitude. To do this, place the bottle cap on the balloon and trace around it with the permanent marker.
- Now draw similar circles centered on the intersections of the equator with the three other lines of longitude. You now have four circles on your globe.
- Add four more circles on the equator that are equally spaced between the four circles already drawn.

- Add a circle on the North Pole (balloon top) and the South Pole (area around the knot).
- Add eight circles in the Northern Hemisphere, about midway between the equator and the North Pole, with two circles between each pair of lines of longitude. *Do you notice that these circles are located on the same line of latitude?*
- Repeat the previous step for the Southern Hemisphere. You now have a total of 26 circles drawn on your globe.
- Examine your globe. *How are the circles distributed? Are the circles on the equator equally spaced? How about the circles between the equator and each pole?* Note that these circles are on the same line of latitude as well. *Are all of the circles equally spaced?*
- Use scissors to snip a tiny hole in the balloon, close to the knot. Allow the balloon to deflate on its own rather than pop it!
- Carefully cut the deflated balloon open along a line of longitude from the South Pole to the North Pole, but stop a little before the very top of the balloon. (Cutting over the very top increases the risk of the balloon ripping when it is stretched out in later steps.)
- Next you will create a projection of your Earth with drawn circles by stretching out the deflated balloon to form a rectangular, flat map. *How do you think the circles will look on your projection?*
- Put the cardboard in front of you on your work area. Place the pushpins within reach.

- Stretch the balloon to be flat and as close to rectangular in shape as possible. (It will be easier with an assistant.) One person can hold one side while the other holds the other side of the balloon. Try to get the equator straight and the lines of longitude as straight as possible. (Note: Do not stretch the balloon too much, as this could rip it.) *How do the circles change in form and size as you stretch the balloon? Also, why would you stretch it into a rectangular shape? Why do you think you should keep the equator and the lines of longitude straight in a projection?*

- Work together to pin the stretched-out balloon onto the cardboard. (Caution: Be sure to put the pushpins in slanted slightly outward, or away from the balloon. Pushpins that are pointing straight down or with the colored tips pointing inward might shoot out due to tension in the balloon.)

- Occasionally a balloon might rip in the process. If it does, hold the ripped edge with your fingers to make the observations. An extra pushpin can sometimes help hold a ripped balloon.

- Examine your flat map, especially the size of the circles. *Are all the circles still the same size? If not, can you find regions on your map where they are?* Remember, all the circles were identical in size on your globe when it was inflated.

- Study your flat map again, now concentrating on the distance between the circles. *Are the circles still the same distance from one another?* Remember, the circles on the equator were equidistant from one another; so were the circles between the equator and each pole. Also, the circles in the Northern and Southern hemispheres were drawn midway between the equator and each pole. *Is this still the case on your flat map?*

- Look at your flat map again, now concentrating on the shapes of the circles. *Do all of the circles still look like circles? Do your observations indicate distortions in your map?* Remember that you started with equally sized circles.

Investigate if the relative direction of the circles, with respect to one another, is maintained in your projection. *How would you describe the direction of a circle with respect to another in terms of north, northeast, etc. on your map? Is this identical to how you would have described the relative direction of that circle to the others on the globe?* If so, the direction has been maintained in that area of your map.

EXTRA

The projection you created is similar to the Mercator projection frequently used to create world maps. Find a Mercator projection world map and compare the size of North America and Africa. *Having done this activity and after looking at the Mercator world map, would you conclude that North America is bigger than Africa, smaller than Africa, about equal in size, or do you not have enough information to compare their sizes?*

OBSERVATIONS AND RESULTS

Were the circles no longer identical in size on the map? Were they still circles?

As parts of the balloon are stretched more than others, the size of the circles is no longer identical on the map. This indicates that relative size and distance are distorted in this projection. Circles on the equator (or any other line of latitude) are still mostly equal in size, indicating that features located on the same line of latitude can be compared in size. Relative to the size at the equator, enlargement gets more prominent as you move away from the equator, and is most extreme at the poles. This explains why Mercator projections can provide misleading information when comparing size or distance. (Note that you cannot extrapolate all of your findings to the Mercator projection. The balloon map you just created shows distortions on the edges that would not appear in Mercator projections.)

On your projection, most circles should still look like circles, indicating that shape is maintained in those areas of the map and directions of the features relative to one another are maintained. In a real Mercator projection, however, the lines of longitude are perfectly straight and direction is exactly maintained, making them particularly useful in navigation.

CLEANUP

Throw away the balloon used for the project. Recycle the cardboard. Put away any other materials used.

Soil Science
How Moist Is That Mud?

CAN YOU TELL HOW MUDDY MUD IS BY ITS COLOR? EXPERIMENT WITH ADDING WATER TO SOIL IN THIS MUDDY ACTIVITY.

Have you ever taken a step onto what appeared to be dry ground, only to find yourself ankle deep in mud? Yikes! When you walk through damp soil, it can be a very messy experience. How can you tell if soil is wet or dry before you step on it? In this science activity, you will investigate whether the color of soil can help you determine how dry or wet it is.

PROJECT TIME

30-45 minutes

KEY CONCEPTS

Soil
Water
Moisture
Colors

BACKGROUND

The amount of water present in a soil sample is called the moisture content. Moisture is very important, and its amount needs to be in careful balance—not too dry and not too wet—for organisms to thrive. Specifically, the soil's moisture content needs to match the needs of the plants, animals, and other organisms living in the habitat. Some organisms, such as ferns and salamanders, need a lot of moisture. Others, such as cacti and some snakes, are adapted to desert habitats and need very little water. Most often, soil with evenly balanced moisture is a haven for plants and small, soil-dwelling animals.

Moisture conditions affect soil structure in many ways, too. Soil that is too wet or does not drain properly can suffer from erosion. That which is too dry can become hard and compacted. Additionally, different types of soil respond to moisture differently. Sandy soil will drain water quickly, but clay soil will prevent water drainage and become soggy.

MATERIALS

- 1 cup of dry soil (Gather this with permission either from your backyard or another outdoor location or from a plant nursery or garden center. If the soil is moist, dry it using an oven, a small baking dish and a cookie sheet following the steps given in the preparation section.)
- Seven identical cups or glasses
- Desk, counter, or table
- Measuring spoons
- Water
- Sheet of paper

PREPARATION

- If your soil is not completely dry, you will have to remove the moisture. With an adult's help, pour the soil into a small baking dish, place it on a cookie sheet then put the cookie sheet (with dish) in the oven and bake it at low heat 200°F (93°C) for two to three hours. This will evaporate the water from your soil. When the soil is dry, carefully remove the cookie sheet and dish from the oven and allow the soil to cool completely.
- Place 2 tablespoons of soil into each of the seven cups or glasses.

PROCEDURE

- Line up the cups in a row on a desk, counter, or table.
- To the far left cup, do not add any water. Into the next cup to its right, add 1/2 teaspoon (2.5 ml) of water to the soil. To the next cup on the right of that, add 1 teaspoon (5 ml) of water. To the following one on the right, add 1 1/2 teaspoons (7.5 ml) of water. Continue increasing by 1/2 teaspoon (2.5 ml) the amount of water you add to each cup as you move to the right; you should end up adding 3 teaspoons (15 ml) of water to the far right cup. *How does the soil in each cup look as increasing amounts of water are added?*
- Now mix the water in with the soil in each cup that includes water. *How do the different cups look as you mix in the water?*
- Place all of the mixed cups on a white sheet of paper. (Placing them on a solid white background will help you compare the colors of the soil in each cup.) Look straight down at the soil in each cup. *Which soil is lightest? Which is darkest? Do you see a correlation between how much water you added and how light or dark the soil is?*

- Now take 1 tablespoon (15 ml) of each soil sample—starting with the dry soil and working toward the one with the most water—and place the sample on a clean area of the paper. Feel the soil with your fingers. *How does each feel? What textures would you expect from each?*
- *Do you think you could use your results to determine the moisture level of other soil samples?*

EXTRA

You could try to quantify the results from this activity by taking a picture of the damp soil in all of your cups, printing the picture out in grayscale, and comparing it with a grayscale color bar (one that has the different amounts of black or white labeled with percentages). *When you quantify your results, just how different are the soil samples? Are some much darker or lighter than others?*

EXTRA

In this science activity, you only tested one type of soil. Try sampling different areas of your yard or another location (with permission) and, without drying them, compare these new samples both with one another and the soil in the original series of cups. *Can you use your original soil series to estimate the moisture content of soil from different places in your yard?*

Try estimating the moisture of soil that is in the same location but on different days. *Does soil moisture change with the weather, such as on hot days compared with cool ones and cloudy days compared with those that are sunny? How much does the moisture vary from day to day?*

OBSERVATIONS AND RESULTS

Did you see that the soil became darker as you added water to it?

Soil color can vary depending on the type that is used but, in general, dry soil becomes darker in color when water is added to it. The color of the dry soil depends on what little particles comprise it—specifically, what minerals and proteins (organic matter) it contains. When water is added to soil, it can replace the oxygen that is naturally in the soil and make the soil darker. This means wetter soil will have less oxygen compared with drier soil. When enough water is added, soil can become saturated and the water will start to form a layer on top of it. You may have seen this happen in the cups with the most water added to them. As mentioned earlier, different organisms need soils with different moisture contents. If the soil is too dry, plants, animals, and microorganisms that need more water will not survive in it, and the soil may also become hard and compacted. If soil is too wet, however, it will not contain enough oxygen for some organisms to survive in it either.

CLEANUP

Put the soil back where you found it, or use it in your own garden. Throw out the muddy paper. Put away other materials used.

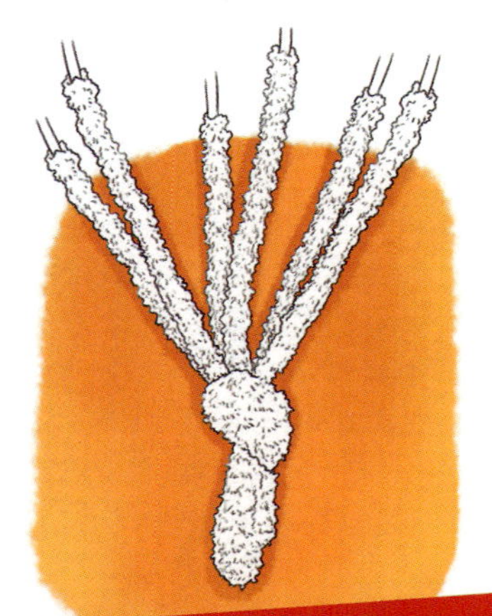

Salt Sculpture Stalactites

TIME TO GET SUPERSATURATED! USE SALT AND BOILING WATER TO MAKE A SUPERSATURATED SOLUTION—AND ADD STRING TO MAKE SOME BEAUTIFUL SALT SCULPTURES!

Did you know you can grow your own crystals at home? You can—and it's easy! Crystals have a definite geometric pattern, and if all goes well, the crystals you grow will be sharply defined, with crisp right angles and smooth faces that vary in size.

PROJECT TIME

2-4 days

KEY CONCEPTS

Crystals
Saturation
Evaporation

BACKGROUND

Table salt is made of many tiny crystals. When you mix these salt crystals with water, they dissolve, losing their crystalline form. When the water evaporates, the salt crystals form once again. The science of crystals, or crystallography, calls crystals shaped like these "cubic." This shape is determined by the way the individual atoms in salt pack together, much as the shape of a pile of oranges would be determined by the way they stack together. Your finished salt crystals should be strikingly beautiful. The key to growing these stunning crystals is quick evaporation—and some string.

MATERIALS

- 1/4 cup of table salt
- 1 cup (237 ml) of water
- About 3 feet (0.9 m) of cotton string
- A saucepan (Enlist an adult's help when working with hot objects and using the stove.)
- Spoon to stir a hot solution
- Cup or small jar (It should have sides at least 5 inches [12.7 cm] high and be able to hold boiling water.)
- Food coloring (optional)
- A tray or plate to hold the cup
- Newspapers or towel to put under the object (optional)

PREPARATION

- Cut the string into six or seven pieces, each about 5 inches (12.7 cm) long, and tie them together at one end so they look like a string bouquet.
- Place the cup or jar on a safe surface where it can remain undisturbed for a few days. Use newspapers or a towel underneath the container to protect the surface if necessary.

PROCEDURE

- To prepare the salt solution, bring the water to a rolling boil in the saucepan.
- Add about a quarter of the salt (optional: and a couple of drops of food coloring). Mix with a spoon to help dissolve. *What happens to the boiling water's appearance?*
- Continue adding and mixing in salt until no more will dissolve into the water. *How much salt were you able to add before it stopped dissolving?* You should now have a "supersaturated" solution. *What does the solution look like now?* You might notice a film of salt crystals forming in a layer on the surface of your solution.
- Turn off the heat and carefully pour the solution into your cup.
- Carefully submerge the knotted end of your strings into the solution, and arrange the strings evenly so that the ends dangle over and around the rim of your cup. *What purpose do you think the strings will serve? Did you notice the strings begin to soak up the saltwater solution?*
- Leave the container someplace where it won't be disturbed.
- Wait and occasionally check in on your crystals. *What do you see happening after one hour? One day? Two days?*

SCIENCE FAIR IDEA

Once the salt solution evaporates enough that it is no longer covering the knot of the strings, you can repeat the above steps and make a new batch of salt solution to add. *What happens over the course of the next day or two?*

SCIENCE FAIR IDEA

Repeat the activity, but this time use different lengths of string, hanging over different objects—at different angles. *How does this change the way your salt strings grow?*

SCIENCE FAIR IDEA

Try to make your crystals different colors by adding food coloring. Make a first batch of salt solution with one color. Wait until the crystals have grown and the solution has evaporated. Now make a second batch with a different color. Add this to the same container without removing the strings. *What happens as this second color evaporates and forms crystals?*

OBSERVATIONS AND RESULTS

When you add salt to water, the crystals dissolve and the salt goes into solution. However, you can't dissolve an infinite amount of salt into a fixed volume of water. When as much salt has been dissolved into a solution as possible, the solution is "saturated."

This saturation point is different at different temperatures; the higher the temperature, the more salt that can be held in the solution. When you boil a batch of saltwater, you cook the salt and water to an extremely high temperature, so the excess salt remains in the solution. However, when the saltwater begins to cool, there is more salt in solution than is normally possible. The solution is therefore "supersaturated" with salt.

Supersaturation is an unstable state, and the salt molecules will begin to crystallize back into a solid. This begins at a "crystallization nucleation" site—such as the fuzzy end of the string. Stirring or jostling of any kind can also cause the supersaturated salt to begin crystallizing.

In a couple of days, you should be able to see that your strings grew fatter from the crystallizing salt. If you continued adding salt solution when it's evaporated below the knot, you should be able to grow long salt crystal stalactites.

CLEANUP

Throw away your salt stalactites. Pour out any leftover water. Put away all other materials used.

Shoreline Science

Exploring the Erosive Energy of Waves

OW DO WAVES SHAPE THE SHORELINE? FIND OUT BY MAKING YOUR OWN MINI BEACH AND SIMULATED WAVES!

A day at the beach is a wonderful way to spend time with your family and friends. You can swim, play games, and build sandcastles. However, have you ever wondered how the beach you are standing on came to be? How, for example, did all of that sand get there? Beaches are formed and continually changed by the ocean's waves moving rock particles onshore, offshore, and along the shore. In this activity, you can investigate how beach formations are made by some parts of a beach that can resist erosion from the waves more than other parts.

PROJECT TIME

30 minutes

KEY CONCEPTS

Oceans
Beaches
Geology
Erosion

BACKGROUND

A beach is a geologic formation made up of loose rock particles such as sand, gravel, and shell fragments deposited along the shoreline of a body of water. A beach has a few key features. The berm is the part that is mostly above water; this is the active shoreline. The top of the berm is known as the crest, and the part that slopes toward the water is called the face. At the bottom of the face, there may be a trough and, further seaward, there may be sandbars parallel to the beach.

The erosion of rock formations in the water, coral reefs, and headlands create rock particles that the waves move onshore, offshore, and along the shore, creating the beach. Continual erosion of the shoreline by waves also changes the beach over time. One change that erosion can cause is the appearance of a headland. This is land that juts out from the coastline and into the water and affects how the surrounding shoreline is eroded.

MATERIALS

- Paint-roller pan
- Measuring cup
- Sand
- Water
- Timer
- Digital camera
- Plastic 16-ounce (500 ml) water bottle (empty)
- Adult volunteer to help take pictures
- Small gravel, such as aquarium gravel

PREPARATION

- Cover the bottom of the paint-roller pan with 5 cups of sand. Build up a beach with most, but not all, of the sand at the shallow end of the pan.
- Slowly pour 6 cups (1.2 l) of water into the deep end of the pan. Let the water and sand settle for five minutes. *How has the beach changed during this time?*

PROCEDURE

- Take a picture of your beach so that you have a record of how it looked in its original state. *Where is the shoreline (the area where beach and water meet)?*

- Lay a plastic bottle horizontally so it is floating in the water in the deep end of the pan.

- For two minutes, bob the water bottle up and down with your fingertips to create waves. If the waves get so big that water splashes out of the pan, make them smaller. *How does the water swirl? How does the shoreline change after one minute? What about after two minutes?*

- After two minutes of bobbing the bottle, take a picture of the beach. *How does it look compared with the first picture?*

- Empty, clean, and dry the paint-roller pan. Prepare a "beach" again, as you did in the preparation section. When the beach is complete, make a "headland" by creating a mound out of 2 cups of small gravel in the middle of the shoreline. The headland should be partly in the water and partly on the beach. Take a picture of the beach with the headland.

- Again, lay the plastic bottle horizontally so it is floating in the water. For two minutes, bob the water bottle up and down with your fingertips. Again, if the waves are so big that water splashes out, make them smaller. *How does the water swirl? How does the shoreline change after one minute? What about after two minutes?*

- After two minutes, take a picture of the beach. *How does it look compared with the previous picture?*

- *How does the headland affect where the water goes? How does it affect how much the shoreline erodes?*

EXTRA

Repeat this activity at least two more times with a ruler taped to the side of the pan. *Exactly how much shoreline erosion occurs with and without a headland?*

EXTRA

Try increasing or decreasing the speed of bobbing the bottle. *Does this affect how the beach changes over time?*

EXTRA

Pour a large volume of water all at once into the deep end of the pan to simulate a storm surge or a tsunami. *What happens to the beach?*

OBSERVATIONS AND RESULTS

Did the shoreline erode, or recede from the water, after you bobbed the water bottle up and down for two minutes? Did most of the shoreline erode less when there was a headland, especially the shoreline closest to it?

As waves hit the shoreline over time, they erode it and push it further inland. When larger and stronger waves hit the shoreline, such as in a storm, more shoreline is eroded. On a beach that is made up of a mixture of small sand grains and larger, dense rocks, the sand will be eroded away first, leaving behind the larger rocks. Over time this can create a headland—an outcropping of the larger rocks—and a bay nearby. The headland receives most of the waves' energy and consequently protects the bay from erosion. Artificial headlands are sometimes created for this purpose: to prevent coastal erosion. In your model, you should have seen that less shoreline eroded near the headland, but further away from the headland, along the sides of the pan, more erosion occurred and the shoreline was pushed farther inland because the more distant shoreline was not as well protected by the headland.

CLEANUP

Dispose of the sand. Rinse out the water bottle and recycle it. Put away other materials used.

Rock Solid?

How Particles Affect Porosity

ROCKS OF DIFFERENT TYPES CAN LOOK SIMILAR IN SIZE BUT WEIGH COMPLETELY DIFFERENT AMOUNTS. FIND OUT WHY IN THIS ACTIVITY!

PROJECT TIME

30 minutes

KEY CONCEPTS

Geology
Porosity
Rocks
Particles

Have you ever heard the expression "solid as a rock"? As it turns out, rocks are not entirely solid. Rocks actually have tiny pockets of air inside them. This is obvious when you look at a piece of volcanic rock (often called basalt), which is full of visible holes. However, dense rocks, such as granite, have tiny air pockets inside them, too. These pockets of air are just much smaller. If you picked up one volcanic rock as well as one granite rock of the same size, you would notice they don't weigh the same. The granite is heavier than the volcanic rock. The many large holes of air in the latter make it less dense—and more porous—than the granite, which also makes it lighter. Something that has more holes in it is more porous. So "porosity" is one characteristic that can help tell you what kind of rock you have.

BACKGROUND

Rocks—and most other objects, for that matter—are made up of particles of varying sizes that are packed together. In between the particles are spaces that are filled with gas, air, or liquid. Particles' shapes and sizes affect how they aggregate, including how tightly they can pack together, which affects a rock's porosity—a property that is the ratio of the volume of a rock's empty spaces to its total volume.

In general, larger particles cannot pack together as well as smaller particles can, which means that packing larger particles together leaves more space for air to fill between the particles. You can imagine this if you have one cup full of marbles and another cup full of sand. You'll be able to see many more spaces between the marbles than between the grains of sand.

MATERIALS

- Three clear plastic cups
- Water
- Measuring cup
- Rocks that can be sorted into one of three size groups (ideally all of the same type of rock, such as granite)
- Screen (optional)

PREPARATION

- Make sure that the rocks are sorted into three different groups by size. The greater the difference in size between the rocks is, the easier it'll be to interpret your results. There should be enough of each group of rocks to completely fill a plastic cup.

PROCEDURE

- Fill each clear plastic cup to the top with one of the groups of rocks. *How much space do you see between the rocks in the different cups?*
- Fill the measuring cup with 1 cup (253 ml) of water.
- Pour the water into one of the cups of rocks, filling the cup to the top.
- *How much water is left in the measuring cup?* Subtracting the amount left in the measuring cup from 1 cup (253 ml) will tell you how much volume the air between the rocks took up. *How much volume did the air take up?*
- To each of the two other cups of rocks, again measure 1 cup (253 ml) of water, fill each cup of rocks with water, and determine how much volume the air took up.
- *How much air did the cup with the largest rocks have compared with the cup with the smallest rocks? How did the volume of air in those cups compare with the volume of air in the cup with the medium-size rocks?*

SCIENCE FAIR IDEA

You can calculate the porosity of each of the cups of different size rocks you used in this activity. To do this, divide the volume of air taken up by each cup of rocks by the total volume of water the cup could hold (without rocks in it). For example, if the air took up 1/2 cup and the cup could hold 1 cup total, the porosity would be 50 percent. *What is the porosity of each of the cups of the different-size rocks?*

SCIENCE FAIR IDEA

Soil is a mixture of rocks, minerals, and organic matter. Porosity is also a property of soil. Try the same activity using different types of soil: clay, loam, sandy, silty, potting soil, compost, etc. Put a screen on top of the cup to keep organic matter from floating out as you pour the water into the cup. *Do different types of soils have different porosities?*

OBSERVATIONS AND RESULTS

Could you see the spaces between the rocks in the cups? Did the cup with the largest rocks have more air than the cup with the smallest rocks? Did the cup with the smallest rocks have less air than the cup with the medium-size rocks?

This activity modeled the inside of rocks on a much larger scale. Because, in general, larger particles cannot pack together as tightly as smaller particles can, a rock made out of larger particles will usually be more porous than a rock made out of smaller particles. However, rocks are not static; like everything, rocks change over time. When enough pressure, or force, is applied to a rock, the pressure can make the rock more efficiently pack its particles. Usually, pressure builds up on rock over a long period of time, as dirt and other rocks end up on top of it. You can see how this process, known as compaction, makes the rock's porosity decrease with time.

CLEANUP

Pour out the water. Rinse and reuse or recycle the plastic cups. Replace the rocks where you found them or use them in your garden. Put away other materials used.

THE SCIENTIFIC METHOD

The scientific method helps scientists—and students—gather facts to prove whether an idea is true. Using this method, scientists come up with ideas and then test those ideas by observing facts and drawing conclusions. You can use the scientific method to develop and test your own ideas!

Question: What do you want to learn? What problem needs to be solved? Be as specific as possible.
Research: Learn more about your topic and refine your question.
Hypothesis: Form an educated guess about what you think will answer your question. This allows you to make a prediction you can test.
Experiment: Create a test to learn if your hypothesis is correct. Limit the number of variables, or elements of the experiment that could change.
Analysis: Record your observations about the progress and results of your experiment. Then analyze your data to understand what it means.
Conclusion: Review all your data. Did the results of the experiment match the prediction? If so, your hypothesis was correct. If not, your hypothesis may need to be changed.

GLOSSARY

aggregate: To collect or gather into a mass or whole.
compact: To press together.
correlation: The state of being associated or occurring together.
counterintuitive: Against what one would expect.
debris: The remains of something that has been broken.
detect: To notice or discover the existence of something.
disintegrate: To break into small pieces.
dissolve: To mix completely into a liquid.
distortion: The act of distorting, or changing something from its natural state.
erosion: The act of wearing away by water, wind, or ice.
extrapolate: To guess about something unknown based on past experience or facts.
friction: The force that slows motion between two objects touching each other.
identical: Being the same.
isolate: To keep apart from others.
perpendicular: Being at right angles.
predict: To guess what will happen in the future based on facts or knowledge.
sensitive: Able to sense or feel changes in surroundings.

ADDITIONAL RESOURCES

Books

Proudfit, Benjamin. *What Do Geologists Do?* New York, NY: PowerKids Press, 2022.

Van Rose, Susanna. *Volcano & Earthquake*. New York, NY: DK Publishing, 2022.

Wood, Alix. *Get Hands-On with Erosion!* New York, NY: PowerKids Press, 2022.

Websites

Discovery Education
sciencefaircentral.com

Exploratorium
https://www.exploratorium.edu/search/science%20fair%20projects

Science Buddies
https://www.sciencebuddies.org/science-fair-projects/project-ideas/list

Science Fun
https://www.sciencefun.org/?s=science+fair

Videos

"Forecasting Earthquakes"
https://ny.pbslearningmedia.org/resource/nvsn5.sci.earth.forecast/forecasting-earthquakes/, PBS Learning Media, 3:39.

"Rising Sea Levels and Erosion"
https://ny.pbslearningmedia.org/resource/rising-sea-levels-erosion-st-catherines-video/georgia-outdoors/, PBS Learning Media, 3:56.

"The Grand Canyon: Its Youngest Rocks"
https://ny.pbslearningmedia.org/resource/ess05.sci.ess.earthsys.anvil/the-grand-canyon-its-youngest-rocks/, PBS Learning Media, 2:01.

INDEX

A
adult helper, 12, 45, 50, 54
air, 25, 57–60

B
balloon, 25–27, 36–41
beach, 17, 23–24, 53–56

C
cardboard, 12–13, 30–33, 36–39, 41
cartography, 35–36
caves, 17, 20–21
chemistry, 17
compression, 23, 26
crystals, 49–52
cups, 6–7, 12–13, 15, 44–47, 50–51, 54–55, 58–60

E
earthquakes, 4–7, 10–12, 14–15, 29–30, 32, 40
engineering, 5, 10–11, 29–30
equator, 37
erosion, 4, 44, 53–56
evaporation, 45, 49–52

G
geology, 5, 17, 23, 53–54, 57

M
markers, 12–15, 25, 27, 30–33, 36–37
moisture, 43–47

P
P-wave, 6, 9–10
paper, 6-8, 12–15, 18–19, 24–25, 30–33, 36–37, 44–47, 50
particles, 23–24, 27, 47, 53–54, 57–58, 60
physics, 5, 11, 17, 23, 29
porosity, 57–60
projection, 36–41

R
Richter scale, 12

S
safety, 29, 50
sand, 4–8, 10, 23–27, 44, 53–54, 56, 58, 60
saturation, 24–27, 47, 49, 51–52
sculpture, 20, 49
shaking, 5–12, 14–15, 26–27, 29, 31, 32–33
soil, 4–6, 9, 20, 43–47, 60
solution, 49–52
straws, 24–27

T
tectonic plates, 6, 30
tray, 6–8, 18, 20, 50

V
volume, 27, 52, 56, 58–59

W
water, 6–7, 9–10, 18–21, 23–27, 43–47, 49–52, 54–56, 58–60
weathering, 17–19, 21, 47
weights, 12–13, 30